Buying Your First Beginner Telescope

How To Avoid Being Disappointed With A Beginner Telescope

Timothy S. O'Connor

ISBN-13: 978-1522838456
ISBN-10: 1522838457
BISAC: Science / Astronomy

DEDICATION

John Dobson

Cincinnati Observatory

Cincinnati Nature Center Astronomy Club

CONTENTS

ACKNOWLEDGMENTS

Carl Sagan, Author C. Clarke, Connie O'Connor, Cincinnati Observatory, Cincinnati Nature Center Astronomy Club, Luis Gabriel Carvajal, Bill LaVine, Nancy Wilson, Aaron Eiben, Matthew Small

In particular I would like to acknowledge Jeff Mancini for his help with this book.

1 DON'T BUY THAT TELESCOPE!

"That which can be destroyed by the truth should be."

-P.C. Hodgell, Seeker's Mask

When I was a young boy I was given a telescope as a present. The box clearly showed brilliant color nebulae, planets in striking detail and amazing claims about the powerful eyepieces and accessories that were included.

I don't know how many nights and hours I tried to find these amazing objects that the box promised I would see but I know it was quite a few.

Eventually, after finding none of the grand views of the planets and deep space objects, I decided the problem must be with me. Apparently science and astronomy were something for which I just did not have the skills.

Over the years I have heard similar stories from many dozens of people whom were given "Department Store" telescopes as children.

It turns out that the "problem" was not in me, my abilities or my dedication, but rather that I and the person who gifted me the telescope were the misled victims of false advertising.

I believe, as do many of my friends who eventually returned to give amateur astronomy a second chance, that this misleading information which is used to market junk scopes is harmful to individuals and to the hobby as a whole.

The good news and irony is that low cost telescopes are available that can be great starter astronomy instruments. Beginners with only basic skills can use these instruments to reveal many hidden treasures of the night sky.

In this book I will provide you with concise informative guides to avoid the pitfalls and misleading marketing when purchasing a telescope or other beginner astronomy equipment for yourself or others.

This is NOT a buyer's guide for specific makes and models of equipment because such guides become quickly outdated and useless. This book will teach you how to determine for yourself what equipment best suites your needs and expectations.

Somehow the market category of telescopes, both beginner and intermediary, has gone under the radar of the "truth in advertising" promoters and lawyers.

The misleading marketing of telescopes is so bad that in my opinion it is even more flagrant than the marketing of "snake oil" alternative medicine products. But at least you won't be spending your health care money on beginner telescopes (that comes later after you are more involved in the hobby).

With some products you can trust that a name-brand version is a good choice, even if you know very little about the product. Unfortunately, that is no help with beginner scopes. Strangely, a large number of high end professional telescope manufacturers make junk toy telescopes and use misleading marketing and advertising for these scopes.

Tell-Tale Indications That You Should Not Buy That Telescope

You don't need to check Angie's List, Snopes, or the Hitchhiker's Guide to the Galaxy to spot the red flags that a telescope is a very bad buy.

The first big red flag to look for is "300x Power," or any Number X-power phrase, as a feature description of a telescope.

This misleading advertising is trying to play off of the common misconception that magnification power is a significant factor in comparing or distinguishing one model or kind of telescope from another. It is not. This kind of advertising is more or less a hoax.

It is true that telescopes do magnify light. However, the magnifications offered on these scopes are useless because of a number of factors, including, but not limited to a scope's size, mount, and functionality.

The "Power of Marketing." If you add up the numbers on the eyepieces of these telescopes, they can magnify to the claimed amount of magnification. However, the actual usable magnification of telescopes this size rarely exceeds 150x under the most ideal conditions.

The principle number on which to grade all kinds of telescopes is aperture, not magnification. In other words, the first characteristic you want to know about any scope is how much light it can gather. This feature is called aperture and is typically expressed or measured in millimeters (mm) or inches.

In general, when it comes to aperture, the bigger the better. All things equal, the more aperture the more you can see and the better you can see it.

Most useful consumer-grade telescopes start at about 3 inches (70mm) and progress up to 16 inches or more.

Our next red flag is when a telescope is bundled with a microscope or some other science-ish toy. Useful telescopes are typically sold with minimal additional equipment such as a mount, eyepieces, and a finder of some kind.

The "look" of the telescope will not be much of a giveaway in most cases. Marketers and producers typically do a good job making products appear superficially like high-grade instruments popular at the time of production.

Price should also be somewhat of an indicator. There are actually some nice useful beginner scopes that are offered at very modest prices. However, expect the lowest-priced scopes to be the least useful.

I am hesitant to put prices in this book as prices change over time but here is a generalized example valid for the time of this writing:

After diligently looking I have found only one useful scope under $100. It is a mini-Dobsonian type and it even has realistic advertising. Other than that one scope expect junk until you progress over $100 and above range.

The next red flag is the size of the eyepiece. Telescopes have removable eyepieces, which come in standardized sizes. Although there are some exceptions to the rule, avoid telescopes with eyepieces smaller than 1.25 inches in diameter. Eyepieces that are .965 in diameter are typically an indicator of a junk scope.

Mount Types

It is critical for a telescope to have a stable mount of some kind, typically either a tripod or what is called a Dobsonian base.

Even if you have good optics, a telescope with a wobbly, light, or loose mount will be completely useless for night-time observing. This fact is often missed or is a surprise to consumers, even those familiar with cameras, spotting scopes or binoculars.

With wide-angle optics such as a camera, spotting scope, or binoculars, the tripod does not have much more work to do than hold the instrument off of the ground. You can "lock down" the tripod and as long as it can keep its payload pointing reasonably well at the target, it does its job.

People familiar with using cheap tripods for cameras and other equipment assume a they will work well for a small, light telescopes. However, this is not true: "apples and oranges," as they sometimes say.

Three ways that a tripod used with an astronomical telescope differs from its use with cameras and terrestrial scopes include: 1. field-of-view, 2. inverted image, and 3. the fact that stars and planets are MOVING targets.

The field-of-view of cameras, binoculars, and most spotting scopes is very wide. This means that if the tripod wiggles, or is bumped, or does not hold exact position, the object is likely still somewhere in view.

With a field-of-view that is not wide, such as found in low-cost telescopes, especially using any eyepiece other than the one with the lowest magnification, the slightest bump, wiggle, or nudge will send the object out of view. To exacerbate the situation, because the view through a telescope is often an inverted or mirrored view, the user will likely push the telescope in the wrong direction to bring the object back into view, making the situation worse and more frustrating.

The next thing that invalidates the experiences of camera, binocular, and spotting scope users is the fact that most of their targets are terrestrial (on the ground). For astronomy, targets are in the sky and always moving as the earth rotates.

In a telescope with a non-motorized mount, the star or other object being viewed will move surprisingly rapidly out of view.

A telescope mount that is adequate for astronomy use will allow the user to smoothly move the telescope to follow a target in the sky without a great deal of frustration.

A stable, heavy tripod increases the cost of the telescope, and again we must be diligent and wary if we are budget minded and want to avoid being the victims of marketing deception.

Experience with camera or spotting-scope tripods will work against you when astronomy-telescope shopping.

There is some good news here, though. Some telescopes in the beginners' market now the aforementioned Dobsonian base or a non-tripod, tabletop base. These bases can be highly stable and effective.

In many cases, tabletop telescope mounts give manufacturers a low-cost way to provide a reasonably stable base as an alternative to a higher-cost tripod.

It is important to realize problems can arise using a tabletop scope if you do not place it upon a sturdy, stable table.

76mm Tabletop Dobsonian Style Telescope

In summary, a very bottom-of-the-line scope is likely to have a series of issues that compound each other in very bad ways. Even if the optics are good, a flimsy tripod will still make it an instrument of annoyance (and vice versa). The good news is you can buy an inexpensive entry-level telescope that has both usable optics and a reasonable mount, provided you know what to look for and are a savvy shopper.

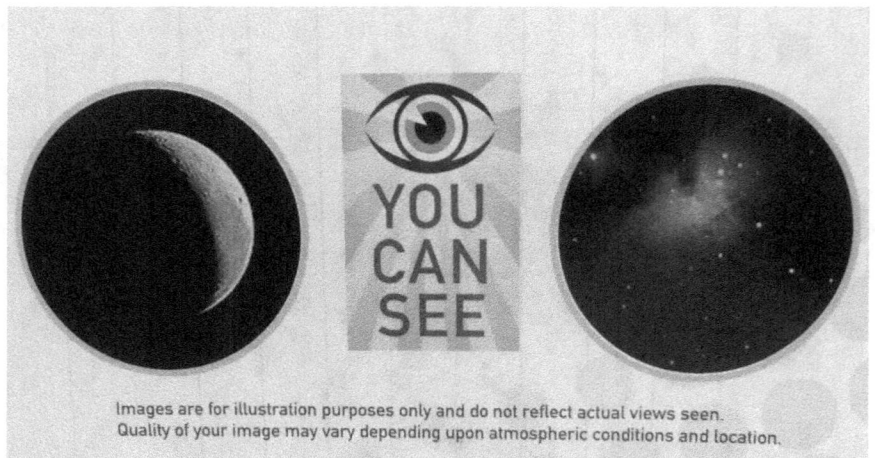

Images are for illustration purposes only and do not reflect actual views seen.
Quality of your image may vary depending upon atmospheric conditions and location.

A conflicting message. The big eyeball "YOU CAN SEE," is positioned between two photos, one of which is the Great Orion Nebula. However, the tiny, fine print, says "Images are for illustration purposes only and do not reflect the actual views seen." Interestingly, this telescope box is better than most, as few even bother with the fine print.

Later chapters in this book will teach you how be a confident, educated, savvy shopper for budget introductory telescopes. These first chapters serve primarily to arm you to avoid the "lies" and marketing fallacies encountered when shopping for your first scope.

The most prevalent misconception about amateur telescopes

Most beginner telescopes will likely have several photos on the box of colorful nebula, giant high-definition photos of planets, maybe Jupiter with its red spot, and even perhaps photos of galaxies and comets.

Color photos of galaxies, nebulae, satellites and planets in striking detail taken from the covers of telescope boxes from local department stores. One photo even appears to be of the sun, which you should NEVER look at with a telescope without special equipment and guidance.

These photos are arguably the most misleading and worst part of the beginner-scope paradox. There are so many ways these photos are misleading about the telescope inside the box, it is difficult to sort out where to begin.

Let's start with the color nebula photos that might even be photos from the public domain library of the Hubble Space Telescope. Amateur telescopes cannot gather enough light for the human eye to see nebulae in color. Even under dark skies in the desert my 16-inch scope costing many thousands of dollars can only see the faintest hues of any color beyond a faint green in the brightest of nebulae. Nebulae, if they can be seen at all in a small scope (3-inch) will appear as faint grey, fuzzy mists.

Enlarged to show detail? The top color photo is the Trifid nebula. To see the Trifid in color as depicted would be difficult to do from professional observatories. Even to get a long-exposure photograph as good as this one would require an advanced and expensive amateur kit.

Next, let's talk about the planets.

Before we start talking about the individual planets, keep in mind that they can be only seen during certain times of the year and sometimes certain times of the night. Finding a good time to view the planets is discussed later in this book.

The bright planets like Venus, Saturn, and Jupiter CAN indeed be seen through a very small telescope. Saturn's rings will be visible even from a city sidewalk with a small beginner telescope. Such a view can be, and often is very inspiring and encouraging as long as you are not disappointed that your view of Saturn is not nearly as clear or in any way as large as the photo on the box.

What does Saturn look like through a small 3-inch telescope? It will look like a bright star with "ears." The ears are the famous rings around the planet Saturn. It will also appear to waver like the planet is under a few inches of moving water. The wavering appearance is from atmospheric distortion and is almost always present unless you are viewing from a remote desert or from a mountain top.

If you have good focus, and reasonable optics, you can watch Saturn for several minutes, noticing that for short instances the planet will become crystal clear. This happens so quickly that you might think your eyes were playing tricks on you or that you just imagined it. However, what you saw was likely quite real and accurate. Every so often the atmospheric disturbance will give a second of clear, undistorted viewing, and this is what you are experiencing.

Jupiter and its moons are also a good target for telescopes of all sizes. Like Saturn, however, it will not appear like the photo that might be printed on your telescope box. Jupiter will appear in a small 2-inch scope like a bright, fat star with some sharp, tiny "stars" nearby. The sharp tiny stars nearby are the great moons of Jupiter. I have been able to see the great red spot in telescopes as small as 5 inches. In 2-inch scopes you might be able to just make out some cloud bands around the planet using a technique called "averted vision" discussed later in this book.

Jupiter tends not to be quite the eye candy that Saturn is, but it can be seen with a small telescope and you can tell it is a planet with moons. Again, how this little wonder is perceived has a great deal to do with your expectations. If your expectations are to see detailed, swirling clouds and a bright red storm on the face of the planet, you are likely to be sorely disappointed. If, however, you are aware of the fact you are seeing with your own eyes, in real time, the King of the planets, and moons that may harbor life, it could be an awesome sight.

Other planets such as Venus and Mars will appear as mildly colored disks through most small telescopes. Venus, in particular, will often exhibit phases or shapes just like our moon. Visual detail will require larger telescopes.

Galaxies will normally not be visible though 2-inch telescopes. Galaxies are mind-bogglingly far away and faint. To make matters worse, galaxies, like nebulae, are easily washed out of sight by even a little bit of light-pollution. Since over 80% of people in North America live under light-pollution too bright to see the Milky Way (our own galaxy), odds are you will need a much larger telescope and better conditions.

The only exception to galaxy viewing is the great Andromeda galaxy. Andromeda is our sister galaxy, and someday it will merge with our own Milky Way. Away from urban lights, and under good seeing conditions, a small 2-inch telescope can see the bright central core of Andromeda, but only as a grey haze. Surprisingly, with a good set of binoculars, you might be able to get a better view of Andromeda's core; more about this technique later. In either case, it will bear no resemblance to any galaxy photos on the box of your telescope. However, it will be the oldest light and the farthest back in time you will likely have ever seen.

If you like a challenge some urban astronomers report being able to see the M94 galaxy under moderate light-pollution .

Photos like this public domain image of M31 is often depicted in astronomy guides and on telescope boxes. However, the human eye cannot see this kind of detail through even the best amateur telescopes.

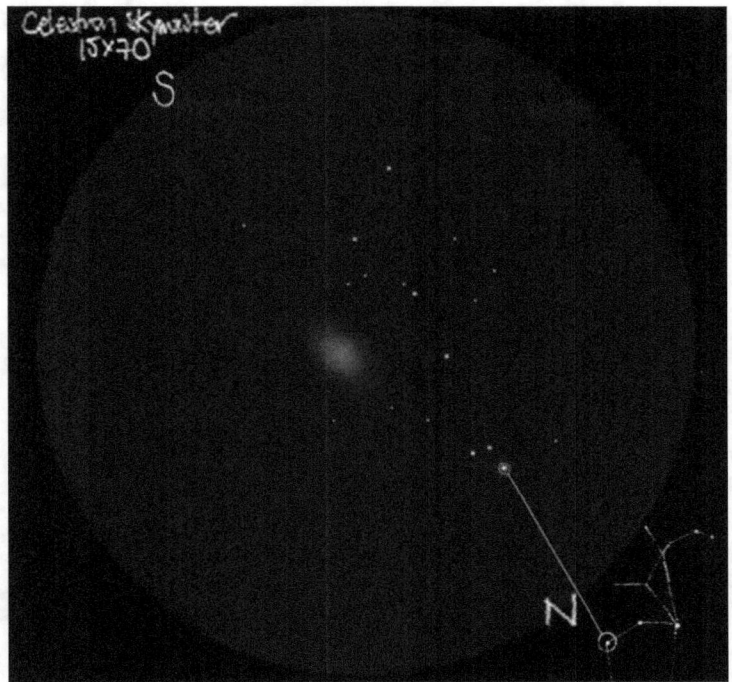

Luis Gabriel Carvajal provides a realistic view of the Andromeda galaxy with this sketch. The observation was done with 15x70 binoculars.

Does this mean you can't see cool stuff with a small scope?

NO!

You CAN certainly see very cool, impressive and inspiring sights through small telescopes!

Telescopically, the recipe for affordable gratification is simple:

1. Avoid the poor quality scopes.
2. Buy a small inexpensive quality telescope.
3. Learn what objects are viewable from your location.

This takes a little more time and learning than just looking at glossy photos on a box but I believe you will find the journey fun and the results very rewarding.

What if the telescope I want to buy is a gift for someone else?

This book provides the knowledge necessary make a purchase that can be the wonderful, valuable gift you intend it to be. There can be no guarantee that a telescope will be the "right" gift for every person young or old, but at least you will be giving a scope that has the ability to do the job should it be put to the task.

So what is the harm in buying a super cheap telescope?

Many people might assume that if the scope is cheap, so what? No harm done; we gave it a shot, and maybe someday we or the person we bought the scope for will get a better, more usable one.

The potential harm is that now a great deal of frustration is associated with astronomy and possibly the sciences in general. According to acclaimed neuroscientist Rick Hanson, our brains are hardwired to retain negative experiences much more strongly than positive ones. So, if you want to inspire someone, you really need to do it right the first time.

You only get one chance to make an impression with a first telescope; be sure it can deliver.

So can you just tell me what I can see with my small budget-scope so I know if it is worth my time to read every chapter in this book?

Well, this is a pretty short book, but okay.

I am going to suggest a very inexpensive reflector telescope with an aperture of about 3.5 to 6 inches. It will not cost much more than department-store telescopes, but it will open up the sky to hundreds of objects. However, if you decide otherwise and buy a scope smaller than 3.5 inches in aperture all is not lost. You will be able to see about a dozen pretty cool sights including the major planets and some great moon features. The planets will not be sharp and crisp like the photos on the box, but views of the moon might!

The Moon is a spectacular object to explore. For telescopes under 90mm (3.5in), it is the primary object for viewing.

The most important things about any size scope that you purchase are that it be of useable optical quality and have a mount suitable for astronomy.

Hurray for the good guys! This telescope ad shows a scope that has usable optics, meets the minimum size needed for backyard lunar viewing, sets good expectations, and includes a moon guide.

What have we learned in the chapter?

1. You don't need "Magnification Power" (330x, 600x etc.) in a amateur telescope. Small telescopes become unusable over 150x. What improves a telescope is aperture. In other words you are looking for light-gathering power, not magnification power.
2. The best optics in the world won't help without a good, steady mount that is easy-to-move to follow the objects in the sky (earth's rotation).
3. Even with a good telescope and a good mount, setting bogus expectations on what you can see with your telescope can be profoundly disappointing. However, with realistic expectations, a small telescope can open up many wonders in the sky.

2 DON'T BUY THAT BOOK!

The previous chapter discussed how many telescope boxes and advertisements can be not only misleading, but completely wrong.

In this chapter, we will deal with the misleading information found in astronomy books/guides, sorting out the information you CAN use.

An Example Story: What I Hope You Can Avoid

I am going to illustrate the principle theme of this chapter using a story about one of my experiences. This experience was one of the things that motivated me to write this book.

One of the popular activities of amateur astronomers is to go on a "hunt" for objects in the sky using a prepared list of deep sky objects. There are a number of these challenges, and the most popular one is called the "Messier Marathon."

Charles Messier was a comet hunter in the 1700s. He made a useful list of deep sky objects he discovered with his 3 and 7-inch telescopes.

I keep a checklist of Messier objects or "M-objects". There are just over one-hundred, and if any are in the sky when I go out to observe, I try finding them.

One summer a few years ago, I found every "M-object" the star charts said were visible from my location during that time of year, except for M97, the "Owl Nebula." According to the description, I should have been able to find the Owl Nebula pretty easily; it is next to the Big Dipper, an easy-to-find constellation which, in fact was directly overhead. By everything I understood, the nebula should be a snap to see because I had a HUGE telescope, a 16-inch telescope called a "Dobsonian." My 16-inch Dobsonian was so large it would not fit in the station wagon, but had to be moved with a trailer attached to the car.

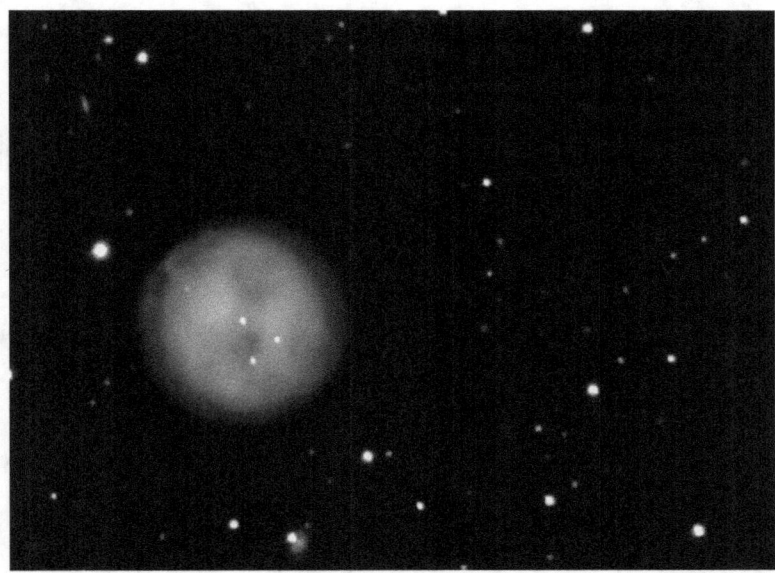

M97, the "Owl Nebula," as depicted in my backyard astronomy guides (Public Domain, Wiki-Commons)

I had several guides on star gazing and they all said pretty much the same thing. Here is an excerpt from the NightSkyInfo web site:

"M97, the Owl Nebula in Ursa Major, is an interesting object for backyard viewing. It lies relatively nearby at 2,300 light-years from our Sun, so it appears 3.2 arcminutes in diameter - only ten times smaller than the Full Moon. The nebula's unusual name goes back to Lord Rosse, who found in 1848 a striking resemblance to the face of an owl, with two dark circular perforations and 'a star in each cavity' giving the impression of two gleaming eyes. This description may sound a little over- imaginative, but if you take a look at his drawing you will see that it's accurate.

Wait until at least midnight to look for this planetary. By then the Big Dipper will have risen high enough so you can see this gem. Trace a line from Beta Ursae Majoris to Gamma, the two stars that make up the bottom of the Dipper's bowl. The nebula lies a fourth of the way along this line and a degree south. While you can see it even with large binoculars, the Owl Nebula remains indistinct even in 6-inch telescopes due to its low surface brightness.

To see the two dark patches that make up the distinctive eyes of the owl, you need at least an 8-inch scope and moderately high power. If the night is very dark and clear you might even spot the central star that appears between the eyes and faint traces of color inside the nebula."

So you can "see it" in just binoculars from your backyard, but if you want to see it distinctly you need a 7-8 inch telescope?

Well I was using a 16-inch telescope, which has 4 TIMES more light gathering power than an 8-inch telescope, and I could see NOTHING. I could not see so much as a slight smudge in the sky.

I tried to view the Owl Nebula night after night, I even tried by computer controlled 10-inch telescope to make sure I was looking in the correct spot in the sky. Nothing. What the heck? Did the owl fly the coop? Was he poached by Orion?

A few weeks later, I traveled to a rural with my 16-inch telescope for a club event. I turned the telescope to where the Owl was supposed to be… and there it was. I could see it! But just BARELY. Even at this "dark" site with a 16-inch telescope, M97 was just a faint, ghostly outline.

According to my "trusty guide," the Owl Nebula could be seen from a backyard with binoculars. Yet, with this giant telescope, nothing could be found.

So what is the deal?

The problem with many, if not most of the books and guides I have purchased or read on the internet, is that they are written from the perspective of someone who is viewing the sky with NO light-pollution and with very good seeing (atmospheric weather) conditions.

The Owl Nebula has low surface brightness, meaning that it cannot be seen with virtually any light-pollution present or under non-optimal atmospheric conditions. Also, the moon must not be in the sky.

I'm not certain, but I suspect many of these guides copy the descriptions from earlier guides. These poor, inaccurate descriptions just keep getting passed down like wives' tales and no longer have any bearing for most of those trying to use them.

According to some estimates, 9 out of 10 people in the United States live in an area where the light-pollution is so bad they are unable to see the Milky Way (our own galaxy) with the naked eye from their backyard. This means that 9 out of 10 people reading these books or online guides will not be able to follow the instructions for seeing M97 no matter how big a telescope they have.

The problem is not only with astronomy guides for amateurs and web pages that copy this information, but also within many computerized telescopes. I have two computerized telescopes from different manufacturers that offer "electronic tours" of the sky. One even has an audio voice that will annotate the tour with interesting science and history facts. About one-third of the objects on this tour are not visible through a large amateur telescope from the average suburban backyard, yet no indication of this limitation is given during the tours.

When you run into these issues, it is easy for someone new to the hobby or even those that have been in the hobby for years to become frustrated and demoralized.

When a telescope manufacturer's guide or a professionally published book or journal makes statements like, "_____ is an object for backyard viewing… can been seen with large binoculars," and despite your best efforts you can not see this object from your backyard with equipment that well exceeds the description given, most people feel they are somehow inadequate for the task of participating in this hobby and their efforts have been a waste.

These content providers should be letting people know that 9 out of 10 people reading this description will not be able to see this object from their backyard and if they can, it will likely be under extraordinarily good weather conditions that only happen a few times a year.

The Great News

Thankfully there are HUNDREDS of very cool things viewable in the night sky from a suburban backyards as well as from urban locations.

The trick is being able to weed out irrelevant, misleading information and find information that is relevant for your location and equipment.

This chapter will include general guidelines on what is visible with certain equipment from urban and suburban locations. Later, this book will list more in-depth resources.

Let's Talk About Equipment Again...

In the first chapter you were advised to <u>avoid</u> telescopes with any of the following features; an aperture less than 70mm (2.75 inches), eyepieces smaller than 1.25 inches, and light tripod mounts that cannot be easily moved to follow the progression of objects in the sky.

Chapter 5 will discuss purchasing recommendations based upon your budget, your location, and whether the scope is for you or a gift.

In the remainder of this chapter, we will cover an introduction to some of the kinds of things you can observe in the night sky with small-aperture scopes, assuming you live, like most of us, in the suburbs or an urban area.

The primary aspects we need to know about your telescope are its aperture and if the mount is GoTo (computer controlled motor-drive). The primary thing we need to know about you is whether you live in the suburbs or in /close to an urban area.

What can I see with my beginner telescope?

Here is what you can see, in general, with beginner telescopes. For more detailed guides see chapter 6.

The moon controls the tides and also what we can view at night with our telescopes. For about two weeks of every month, the moon and the bright planets are about the only things we can see well from an urban or suburban backyard.

The approximately two weeks of the month when the moon is not in the night sky or is only slightly illuminated by the sun, give us a chance to see some of the less-bright objects in the sky called Deep Space Objects (DSOs).

If you have a telescope smaller than 70mm (2.75 inches), your primary object of night viewing will be the moon. At certain times of the year, you will be able to see the bright planets, but unable to see much detail.

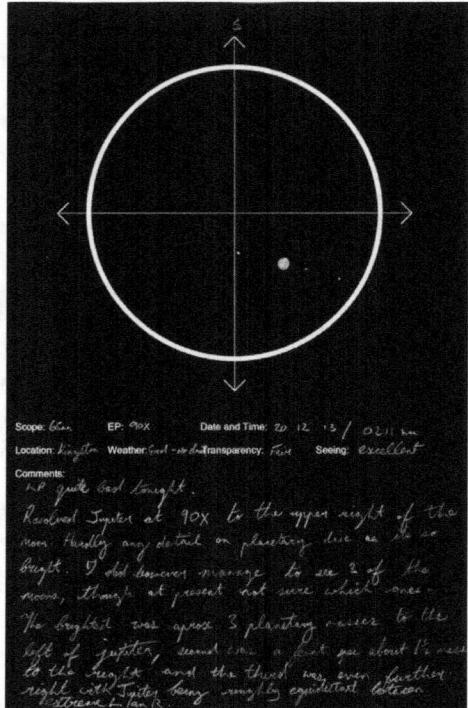

A telescope less than 70mm (2.75 in) may not to allow you to see distinctive cloud bands on Jupiter, but you should be able to make out Jupiter's moons and Saturn's ring. (Sketch by Matthew Small, using 65mm telescope)

If you have a telescope that is 70mm to 90mm (about 3 to 4 inches), much more can be seen in the night sky.

With 3-4 inch telescopes in a suburban or urban backyard you can make stunning observations of the moon. The moon has quite a few surprising features and remarkable vistas, especially if you know a little about what you are observing or looking for. Chapter 6 will list several guides to the moon that can potentially give you many hours, if not years, of challenges and quests in moon-observing.

Another advantage to moon observations is that they are highly tolerant to light-pollution , poor seeing conditions and even some weather.

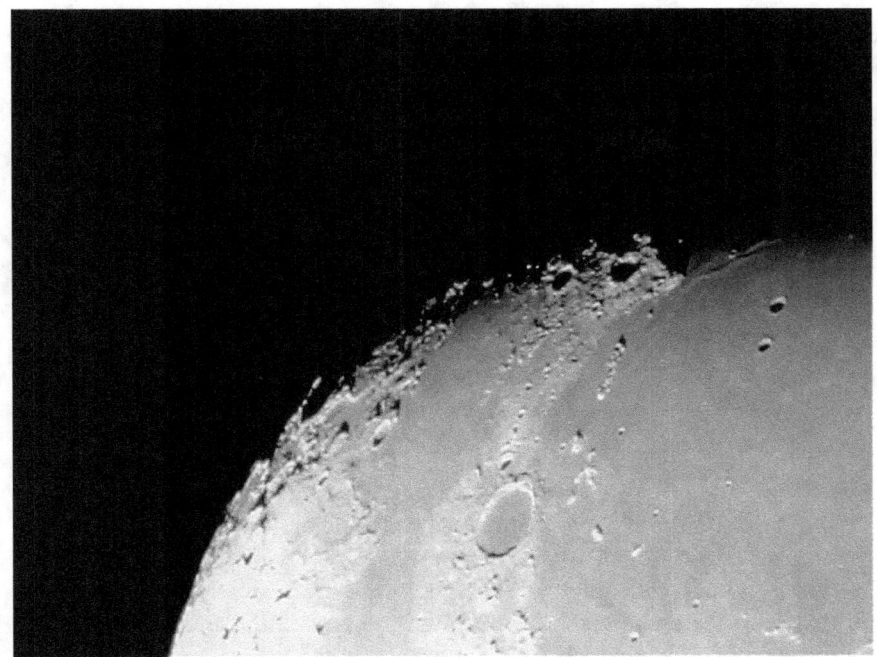

The views of the moon are highly tolerant to atmospheric conditions.

If you check your calendar and star charts, most times of the year one of the bright planets should be available for viewing.

With 3-4 inch telescopes, Saturn will have a well-defined ring system; Jupiter under good seeing conditions will show some cloud banding, and its big moons will be viewable like tiny, nearby stars.

You will be able to see Mars and Venus with 3-4 inch scopes, and tell they are planets, not stars. However, it is unlikely that you will be able to see any surface or cloud detail.

One of the biggest advantages upgrading to 3-4 inch scopes is that you have the ability to view a few of the Deep Space Objects (DSOs).

Keep in mind that Deep Space Objects are mostly "fuzzy, grey smudges" that are challenging to locate and observe. The fun in DSO viewing comes primarily from knowing some facts about what you are trying to observe and the satisfaction from completing the challenge.

DSOs demand that you pay close attention to the calendar, weather, viewing conditions, and moon phases and develop some skills for finding your way around the night sky and constellations.

If successful, you will see a small, grey smudge or what looks like a tiny cloud in your eyepiece just on the edge of visibility. That might not sound like much, but if you know some facts about what you are viewing your perception might change. If you know the kind of strange space object you are viewing, or how old the light is that is hitting your eyeball and that you are seeing it LIVE in person and not just some photograph, many people, like myself, find this hugely rewarding, and eventually addicting.

Two of the more notable DSOs you can see from the suburbs with 3-4 inch telescopes are the Ring Nebula (M57) and the Great Orion Nebula (M42).

The Ring Nebula looks unique, like a grey smoke ring or a ghostly donut. When you look at the Ring Nebula, in a way you are looking at the past and the future. The light you are looking at is 2,200 years old and the object you are looking at is an exploded sun that was very similar to our own sun. Someday, a few billion years from now our sun will die and form a nebula that will likely look similar to this one.

The Ring Nebula is in the constellation Lyra and can take some practice to find. Remember that it is not always visible, especially if there is a great deal of humidity in the air. Keep trying. Generally it is best found when high in the sky during the summer with a medium eyepiece. In a low-power eyepiece, it might be mistaken for a dim star.

If you have a computerized GoTo telescope, it will take much of the guesswork out of finding DSOs. However, you won't learn to navigate the stars.

The Great Orion Nebula is easy to find. This huge nebula is located around the sword in the easily identifiable winter constellation Orion. On nights with poor seeing, or in urban environments, it will look like automobile headlights driving through fog. With a larger telescope,
in the suburbs on nights with good seeing and no moon, it will look like a grey and black veil vaguely in the shape of a bat or wing. Always use the lowest-power eyepiece to view this nebula.

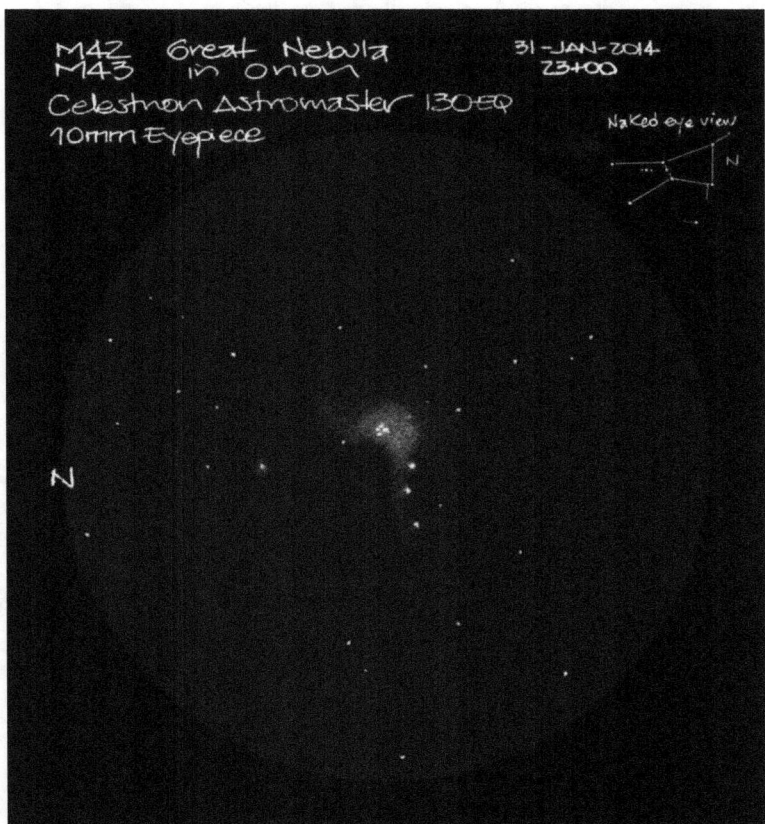

The Orion Nebula is a large bright deep space object. Luis Gabriel Carvajal's sketch above shows what you can expect to see through a 5-inch telescope under good viewing conditions.

Low Power Ocular

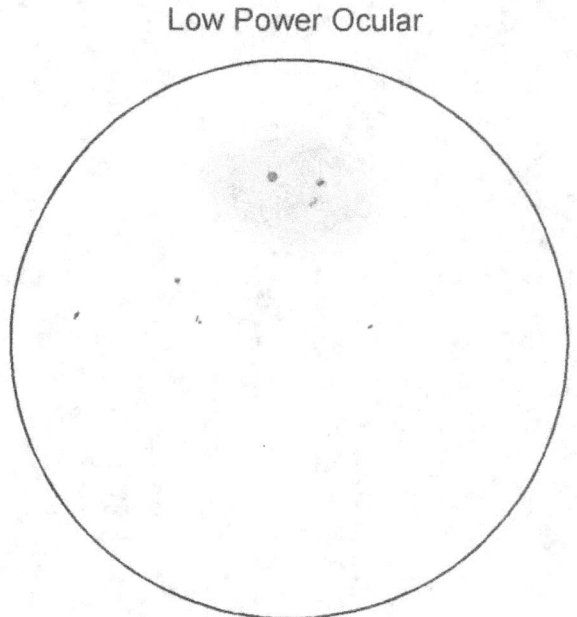

Under suburban skies with a small telescope, the typical view of the Orion Nebula will look like a pair of car headlights in fog.

The Orion Nebula is massive, and its scale is hard for the human mind to really grip. This nebula is over twenty light years across and is a nursery for newborn stars. The Orion Nebula has been, and still is, one of the most intensely studied objects in the sky with lots of scientific secrets yet to yield.

Telescopes with 3-4 inch apertures tend to be very portable. The best telescope is the one that you use most often; and having a scope that is easy to set up, put away, or grab and take on a vacation is a great advantage. Some of the most desirable and famous amateur telescopes in history fall into this size class such as the Meade ETX-90, Edmond Astroscan, and the Questar.

The next step up are the 4-6 inch telescopes, the top end of the beginner scopes.

As you might expect, you can see more objects with these scopes than the scopes smaller than 4-inches in aperture. Specifically, the most important improvement gained by upgrading to these scopes is the greater amount of detail you see when viewing objects.

If you are buying a 4-6 inch telescope, you want to have some indication that you or the person you are buying the telescope for has a reasonably keen interest in astronomy and is likely to pursue the hobby. Not all, but most of these scopes are not as portable as the 3-4 inch scopes and will take up a bit more real estate in the closet or trunk.

With 4-6 inch scopes, you will be looking at mostly the same objects as with a 3-4 inch scope. Everything will be brighter and more detailed and you might get a chance to use a high-power eyepiece.

Viewing Saturn, you will have a fair shot of seeing the Cassini Division, an indicator that you are seeing the separation between the great rings. With Jupiter, you may get a good chance to see the famous Great Red Spot. However, as of this writing, the Great Red Spot is slowly turning into the great pale spot and becoming much harder to see against the adjacent clouds in Jupiter's atmosphere.

On good nights away from suburban lights you might be able to see some of the planetary nebulae other than the previously mentioned Ring Nebula, such as the Eskimo Nebula and Blue Snowball. Beware, these objects look like dim stars until using a higher magnification.

Galaxies are still going to be largely washed out by the suburban sky-glow with the exception of the previously mentioned Andromeda galaxy and perhaps M94. Andromeda's central core will still be the only visible structure. M94 has a very high surface brightness and might appear similar to the globular clusters discussed in the next paragraph. The best time to find M94 is in the spring when it is high in the sky.

Other than the planets, star clusters are the only other significant upgrade in viewing you get with 4-6 inch scopes. The brightest star clusters, including the Hercules Globular Cluster, are like dwarf galaxies just outside our galaxy and are even gravitationally bound to the Milky way.

Under suburban skies, with smaller scopes most of the globular star clusters look like a grey smudges. However, as you approach about 5 inches of aperture, you start to get enough resolving power to see these Deep Space Objects as groups of glistening stars like diamonds piled up on a black velvet tablecloth.

Globular Clusters are very dense groups of stars, similar to dwarf galaxies. Most will look like dim fuzz balls, but under good seeing conditions with a 125mm or larger scope, a few will begin to look like diamond piles on a black velvet cloth, even from suburban locations. (Sketch from Binoculars, Luis Gabriel Carvajal)

Hopefully we are now armed with the knowledge we need to "myth-bust" bad information from some astronomy books, guides and web pages. In chapter 6, we will learn where to find good guides to the heavens, but now we must move our myth-busting activities on to telescope accessories in the next chapter.

3 FILTERS AND OTHER ACCESSORIES

Under the assumption that you have or will have a small budget-telescope, there are some accessories that you may want to consider and also some that you may want to avoid.

Some telescopes marketed to consumers as beginner scopes come with "bundled accessories." If two scopes seem roughly equal, should you base your decision on the included accessories?

Or, perhaps you are buying your first scope; what accessories should you buy to go with it?

Like the marketing of telescopes, accessory marketing can also be misleading, but thankfully, usually not to such a great extent.

Eyepiece filters are a good starting example.

Many telescopes have bundled with them a set of four or more eyepiece filters, typically four color filters and a moon or lunar filter.

You can go ahead and discard the colored filters.

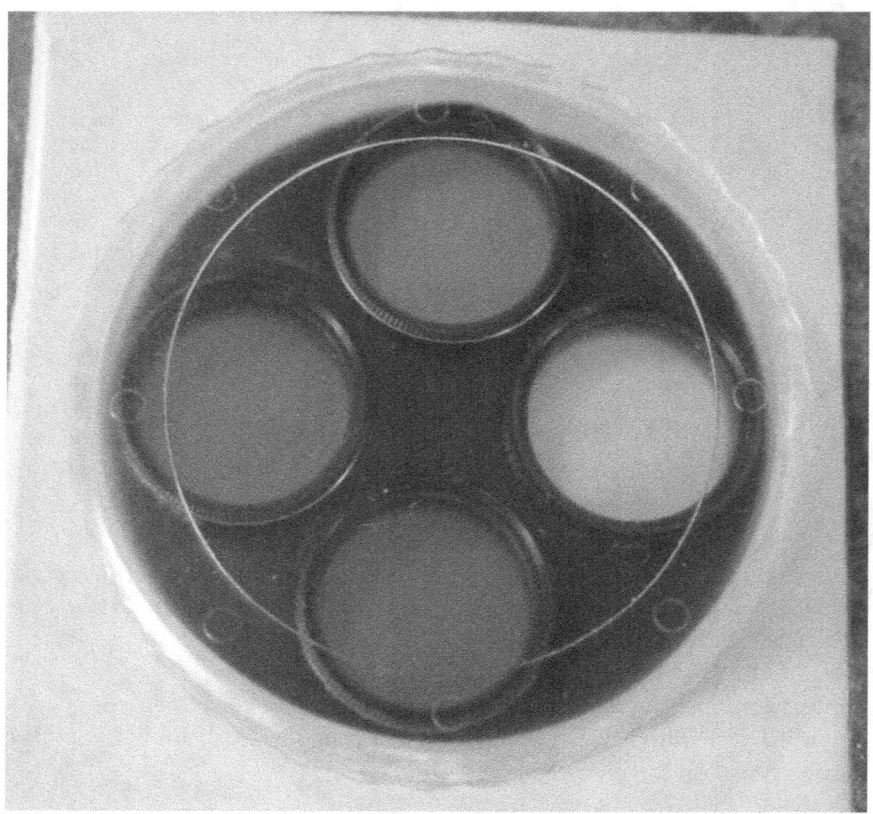

Basic color filters tend to be the least used filters. Don't make a telescope buying decision based on the addition of this accessory.

The most common misconception about filters is that they let you see more. No! Filters filter OUT light. What do small telescopes fall shortest on? Light gathering ability. Do you see the problem?

Do not throw out the lunar/moon filter though; that will come in handy.

With only a few rare exceptions, filters are useless to a beginner with a small-aperture telescope unless looking at the moon and then only the lunar/moon filter is required.

Filters block out certain colors or wavelengths of light to make other colors or wavelengths stand out or have more contrast.

In a small telescopes there's no light to spare. Period.

If there is light to spare, as with larger telescopes (8 inches or larger), you would likely purchase very specialized filters to view very particular kinds of objects, or for photography. These filters tend to cost almost as much, or more than, many beginner telescopes.

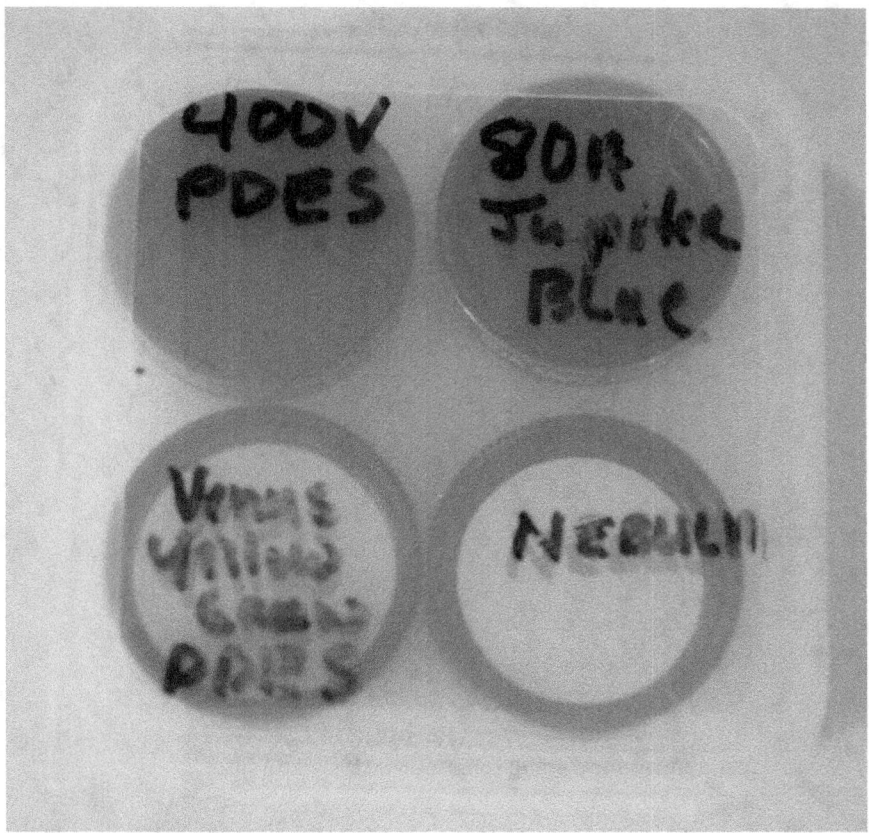

Filters take away light, not add to it. Specialty filters are typically of little use in small telescopes six inches or smaller and can cost as much as a beginner telescope.

The big exception to this is the lunar or "moon filter."

The moon is so bright that it can be difficult to view with a telescope and may even be so bright as to cause your eyes to water.

The moon filter reduces the amount of light so you can view the moon without having to squint at the eyepiece. As this book has mentioned, and will expound on later, the moon is one of the principle targets for small scopes and urban astronomers.

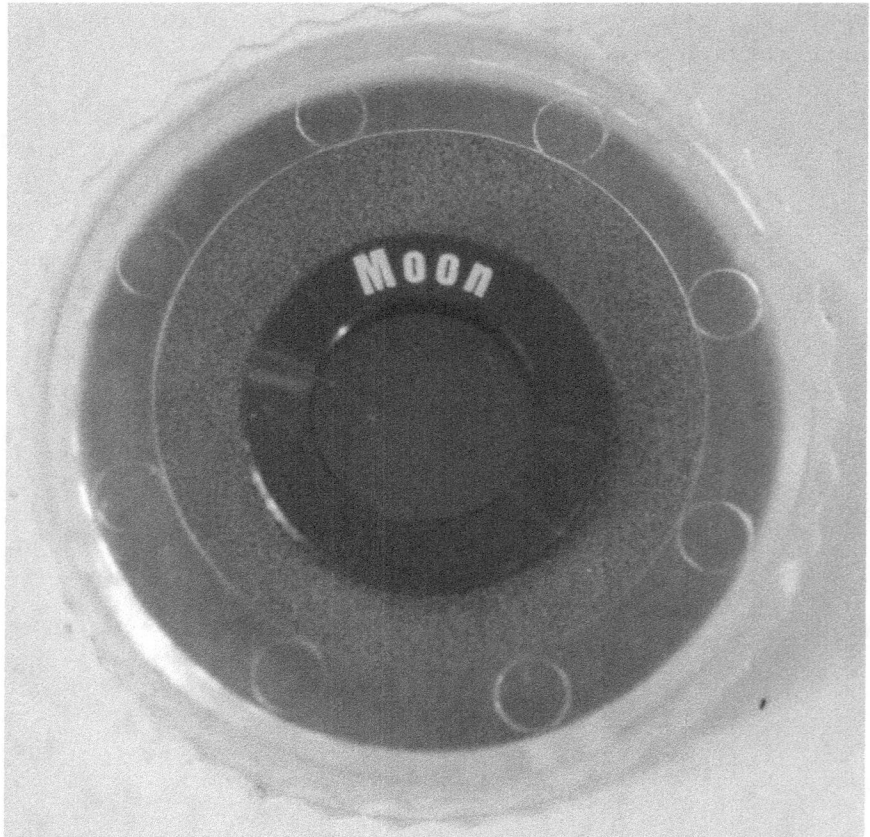

The most useful filter for a small telescope— the moon filter.

Typically the lunar filter included with small scopes has a fixed amount of light blockage. It works, but it will block the same amount of light whether the moon is full or just a sliver. If you, or the person you are giving the scope to, are considering using the telescope for a fair amount of lunar observing, you may look into upgrading to a variable polarizing filter.

A variable polarizing filter consists of two filters that when rotated allow you to control exactly how much light passes through them. This allows you to set the amount of light and contrast that looks best for the phase of the moon you are currently viewing. At the time of this writing, a new, no-name variable polarizing filter on eBay costs about $20.

If later you acquire a larger telescope, the variable polarizing filter might help add contrast to bright objects like Jupiter, Saturn, and Venus.

Solar filters can give a wonderful view of the sun, exposing sunspots and the surface of the sun. Misuse of a solar filter can instantly blind you, so I will not be recommending solar filters in this book for new astronomers. I do need to give you an important warning, however. If you have an old vintage telescope with a solar eyepiece filter, **dispose of the filter at once**! These old filters will break in the heat of the sun without warning and blind anyone looking through it. Use only modern filters and seek the advice of professionals before using solar-viewing equipment.

The promises of seeing something new or better are hard to ignore. If you are sorely tempted to buy a filter, I recommend you make some friends in a local amateur astronomy club and ask to borrow a filter, or let them show you a filter through their telescope.

Remember, if you use a filter when looking though a larger telescope, the filter is going to perform many times better.

Light-gathering works like this: 3.5-inch telescopes gather three times as much light as 2-inch telescopes, 8-inch telescopes gather over five times as much light as 3.5 inch telescopes. In addition to the increased light, additional resolution or detail is possible at higher magnifications. Most common filters only start to make a really helpful view modification in 8-inch or larger scopes.

Filters must be stored and handled carefully, so you may want use those unused color filters as practice for handling and using filters before working with the more expensive and more useful filters. You definitely want to practice this before borrowing any from your friends.

Planets are some of the best targets for small scopes, so it is pretty tempting to purchase filters that advertise enhanced planetary viewing. I don't want to discourage an exploration of filters, but it is good to keep in mind that many other accessories would also love to be included in your budget.

Should you decide to explore filters, you might ask a friend to demonstrate a medium blue Jupiter filter.

A special medium blue filter sold by some quality astronomy dealers can help you find the Great Red Spot on Jupiter. The filter will NOT make Jupiter look better, rather it will cause the Great Red Spot to stand out on the planet. This can help you find the GRS when you think you see the spot with no filter and want to confirm. These filters run about $20. However, if Jupiter is not bright enough in your scope, or Jupiter is very small in apparent size, the filter is likely to just make Jupiter look like a little blue blob.

A blue filter can help you find the Great Red Spot, but does not make Jupiter more attractive or brighter. The dark region on the lower left is the GRS. This photo was taken with a 125mm SCT Telescope. To the human eye looking into the eyepiece, Jupiter would look much smaller. Remember, photographs typically provide better views than the human eye.

This image simulates the size and view of Jupiter in a 125mm (5-inch) telescope under suburban conditions— Blue filter on the left, no filter on the right. The blue improves contrast, making the GRS more visible. Keep in mind the planet image will not be still. The planet will appear to waver like a coin viewed under water at the bottom of a small stream.

Eyepieces and Barlows

Most new telescopes come with eyepieces and possibly Barlow lenses as included accessories.

Eyepieces with good optical quality and a wide field-of-view are expensive so good quality telescopes typically come with only one or two eyepieces with the assumption that the customer will buy additional eyepieces depending on their needs and preferences.

"Department-store" telescopes will often come with two or three eyepieces and sometimes even something called a "Barlow". The telescope marketer is likely trying to make the telescope appear more appealing than the higher-quality competition by including more "accessories. Unfortunately, it is likely the eyepieces are of poor quality and have magnifications and field-of-views that are nearly useless for the resolution available though that telescope.

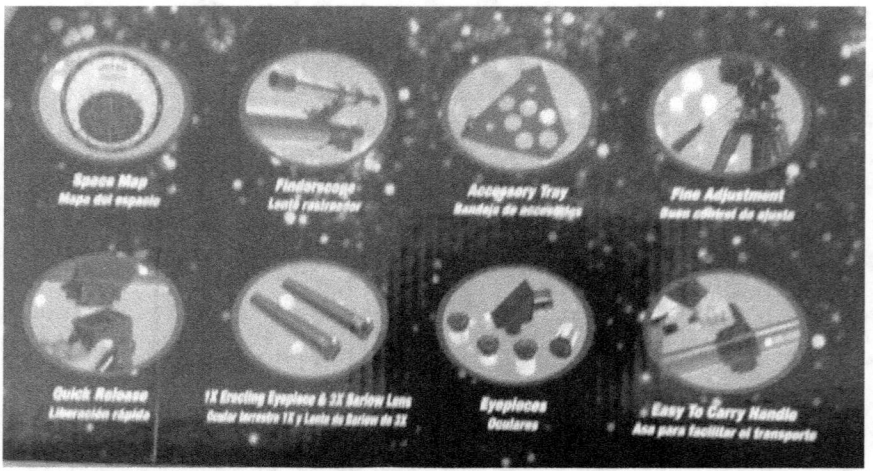

Beware of excessive accessories such as Barlow lenses and three or more eyepieces. Typically, good telescopes are bundled with only two good quality eyepieces.

The Barlow lens is a holder that you can fit an eyepiece into that doubles the magnification of the eyepiece. The Barlow improves the magnification but not the view, especially in small telescopes. It does, however, let marketers of a low quality telescopes claim twice as many "powers."

The work-horse eyepieces of a telescope are the low-power, wide-field eyepiece and the medium-power eyepiece. Remember it is a common misconception that magnification is what is desirable in a telescope; what is most useful is light gathering ability and good optics.

Higher quality beginner telescopes will have various configurations. Typically they will include a 20 or 25mm eyepiece with a 1.25-inch barrel, and sometimes an additional 9 or 10mm eyepiece.

Somewhat counter-intuitively, the 20mm eyepiece will be the low-magnification eyepiece and the 10mm eyepiece the high-magnification.

Having astronomer friends, or a club in town, can be a great help because you might be able to ask them to put their eyepieces in your scope to see what views you can see before purchasing any additional eyepieces.

With a small scope, it is unlikely you would want to go to an eyepiece with a higher magnification than what you get with your 9 or 10mm stock eyepiece. Generally, an eyepiece in the low-twenty-millimeter range, and another under 15mm, will be all you need to enjoy your scope.

Useful Accessories That Are Not Typically Bundled With The Scope

The scope most used is the best telescope to own. A soft or hard protective case that allows easy transportation can be a fantastic investment if it helps taking your telescope to more viewing locations such as vacations and star-parties (club events). Cases serve to protect the optics when not in use.

Depending on the design of the telescope, a dew shield or dew heater might be required for humid nights. Dew heating systems tend to be much more expensive and require a power supply, so the most likely choice for a new small scope would be a dew shield of some kind.

If after using the telescope for a while the view turns hazy, shine a light on the front lens or main mirror inside the telescope to check for dew. With many small scopes, you can make your own home-made dew shield out of foam or construction paper.

You will want a star chart (map of the sky) or a tablet / smart phone app with a star-chart function. If you have a GoTo or PushTo telescope, you will want the chart for initial alignment. If you have a manually operated scope use the chart to locate objects using a technique called star-hopping.

Rotating star finders are just a few dollars, and are a good way to learn the night sky. They are available in many sizes and will help you understand how the night sky appears to move.

In general, flashlights and other light are to be avoided during an observing session. However, they are sometimes needed for reading charts or finding dropped objects. It is important that your flashlight be DIM. A bright flashlight will instantly remove the dark adaption of your eyes, and diminish your viewing ability considerably. You can buy a dim red flashlight from many dealers or just make your own using paint or red cellophane over the front of the flashlight.

It is desirable to clean the glass on your eyepieces and telescopes as little as possible. If and when you do get a finger print or a smudge on your glass, NEVER use a paper towel or tissue to clean the lens. Always use a microfiber lens cloth, or in a dire emergency, a very clean 100-percent cotton-cloth.

A writing instrument and note or sketchpad can also be wonderfully helpful. Making a list of what you found, what it looked like and what you could not find will increase your observational skills.

Nearly all telescopes are equipped with a finder scope. Finder scopes help aim the telescope at the target in the sky that you plan to view. On many newer scope models, finder scopes have been replaced with "red dot" finders like those used on some firearms. These red-dot finders work well, and many people prefer them to optical-lens finder scopes.

As previously mentioned, if you have a tabletop telescope, you will need a good solid table. If you are using another kind of mount, you will want a chair or stool. One challenge to finding the right stool is, that as the telescope points to different parts of the sky, you may want a higher or lower seating position. A common solution to this is to use a step-stool ladder with wide steps that can be used as seats.

4 COMETS

Comets are one of the most exciting things to view in the night sky.

When "Great Comets" such as Halley's and Hale-Bopp appear, telescope sales go through the roof. That is not such a bad thing, I think, as long as those sales are motivated by an interest to see the night sky in general.

The critical thing to know about bright naked-eye comets is that you don't want to use a telescope to observe them.

Naked-eye comets are large, diffuse objects that cannot be seen well through a telescope. The best instrument for viewing them is a set of binoculars, preferably astronomy binoculars mounted on a tripod or something called a "parallelogram mount."

Binoculars will have enough field-of-view to see the comet and its tail. Despite their low magnification you will be able to see subtle tail details and from a dark site, perhaps some hints of color.

With a telescope, the comet tail will be difficult or impossible to fit into the field-of-view and it will have less contrast at the higher magnification. The telescope will possibly see more detail in the area of the comet nucleus, which is interesting but not what most people want to see when viewing a great comet.

A comet seen through a telescope gives a great view of the coma and nucleus, but telescopes do not give pleasing views of comet tails. (Lovejoy Q2, O'Connor)

Naked-eye comets are rare, fabulous sights and if one does become visible in the night sky, you really should make a special effort to view it with a set of good binoculars from a location away from city lights.

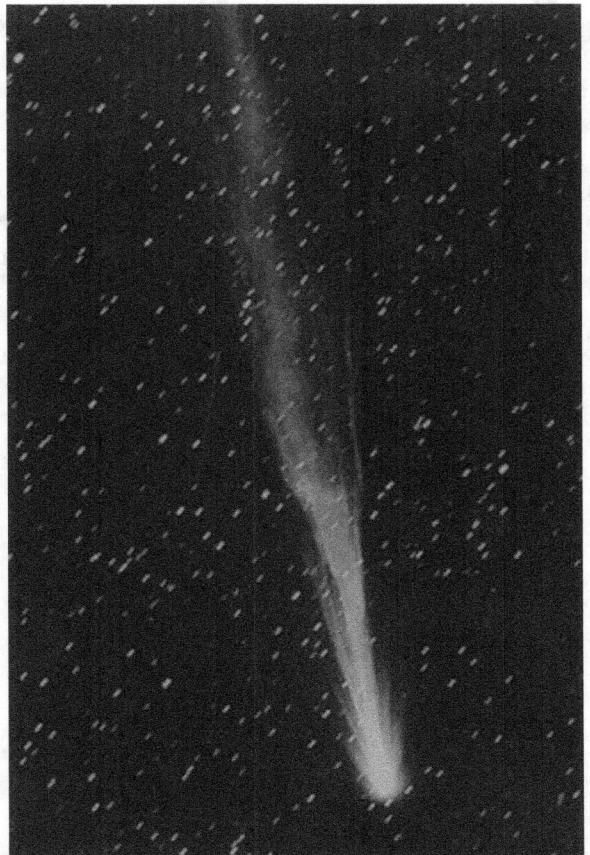

Comet tails are best seen in photographs or very low-power wide-field views. (Public Domain)

Many people do not realize most years have three or four comets that are not visible to the naked eye, but often can be viewed with small telescopes.

Comets visible with telescopes tend not to have tails, or if they do, the tails are visible only in long-exposure photos. They look like misty balls in space. Because most visible comets will not return again in our lifetimes, many amateur astronomers really enjoy hunting them.

Comets are not easy to observe as they are hard to see in light-polluted skies and tend to be hazy, indistinct objects. However, like any challenge, there tends to be a sense of reward and achievement when locating one knowing, that only a handful of humans will ever see it with their own eyes.

To locate these telescopic, bright comets, it is best to check several websites that post updates and track these objects. As we have covered in previous chapters, the descriptions given about what equipment is required to view these comets assumes a viewing location free of light-pollution .

Comets can be discovered sometimes only weeks before the best time to observe them, so it is a good idea to frequently check these sources. To find websites that track this information, use your search engine to query the term "Visible Bright Comets."

Comets have an amazing history of influencing our cultures and history, much of which is documented in Carl Sagan's book *Comet*.

5 WHAT KIND OF SCOPE TO BUY

As previously covered in the first chapter, avoid telescopes with poor optics and mounts.

Now that we know what not to buy, what *should* we buy as a first telescope?

Usually, budget is the limiting factor. This book assumes, for your first telescope, or for your telescope gift-giving, that keeping the price down is a significant concern. That said, the smallest usable scope recommended by this book is 70mm (2.75 inches).

In the world of telescopes, the more aperture the better, so much so that there is a common term in the hobby called "Aperture Fever". Aperture Fever is the seemingly never-ending quest to get a larger telescope to see new objects and to see familiar objects with more detail.

There is one exception to the aperture rule —portability, or rather, lack of. You tend to favor the scope that you use the most. A scope that is hard to transport or setup gets used less often.

There is a special "Goldilocks Zone" where aperture and portability meet and in this zone are the most notable and popular amateur telescopes ever made.

It is not uncommon for owners of large expensive scopes to also have a cherished second telescope in the Goldilocks Zone that is typically referred to as a grab-and-go telescope.

As we have previously learned, sky conditions, location and timing have a great deal to do with good astronomy and viewing. Having a telescope that is highly portable and also large enough for good visual observations is a wonderful tool.

The Goldilocks Zone for grab-and-go telescopes is between 90mm and 125mm (3.5 to 5 inches).

The most famous telescopes known to the hobby of amateur astronomy fall into this zone, including the Meade ETX-90 and ETX-125, Edmond Scientific AstroStar, and Questar 3.5 series.

Some small, high-quality telescopes have what amounts to a cult following. Pictured here is a Meade ETX 125.

The Questar telescopes were the first commercial telescopes to take off as high-quality grab-and-go telescopes. Famous scientists and celebrities are well known for singing the praises of these compact, yet useful, telescopes such as Vernher Von Braun, Johnny Carson, Marlon Brando, and the inventor of the communication satellite, Arthur C. Clark.

Arthur C. Clark wrote the following about his Questar:

"I had brought with me, for just such a purpose, the finest small telescope ever built--the 3-1/2 inch Questar, a jewel of precision optics which has produced close-ups of the moon that could easily be mistaken for Mount Wilson photographs. Although the barrel is only eight inches long, a combination of lens and mirror makes the light traverse the tube three times, with the result that the instrument is equivalent to one yard in length. Various eyepieces give magnifications of up to 180, though it is easy to go higher than this on those rare occasions when the clarity of the atmosphere permits. There is an electric drive in the base that will keep the field of view centered on a star all night--no, I am not getting a penny from the Questar Corporation, but perhaps I had better stop here."

The Questar telescopes are now considered collectors' items and fetch too high a price to be considered for a beginner's telescope. At the time of this writing, good, used Questars are going at auction for more than two-thousand dollars.

Meade and Edmond Scientific both entered this market after Questar with lower cost grab-and-go scopes. The Meade and Edmond Scientific telescopes are mass produced telescopes of good quality.

Today the choices are even greater as small Dobsonian and tabletop grab-and-go telescopes offer even more affordable options.

In this book we will try to avoid recommending specific makes and models of telescopes because such books are quickly outdated.

Telescope Designs

Nearly every single book on astronomy explains the principle types of telescope optics.

I am not going to repeat that information here; it can be found for free with much better illustrations than I can provide with a quick search on the internet. However, I will talk about the pros and cons of each design from the perspective of a beginner telescope.

ReFRACTors.

Refractor telescopes, unfortunately, are the most common design marketed to beginners. These telescopes are shaped like pirate spy-glasses.

Refractors are simple to assemble, and low-cost (low-quality) lenses are readily available to manufacturers. Therefore, the bulk of junk, beginner telescopes are refractors. There are some excellent-quality beginner refactors that can be found at the high-end of the price range, but it takes some careful research to make sure they are of usable optical quality.

ReFLECTors.

Reflectors use mirrors to direct light into the eyepiece, hence "reflect" in the name.

Mirrors provide the most "bang-for-the-buck" in terms of light gathering, a critical factor to pay attention to.

If your first scope will be on the middle or lower end of the price spectrum, the majority of your choices will be Newtonian Reflectors.

Cassegrain

Schmidt and Maksutov Cassegrain telescopes are hybrid reflector AND refractor telescopes and are the most popular type of high-end grab-and-go telescopes.

Cassegrain telescopes are like a hybrid of reflector and refractor technology because they have a corrector lens and a mirror.

Cassegrain (SCT, Mak) telescopes are small, highly versatile telescopes that often have built-in motors, or even computer controllers, to aid in finding and viewing astronomical targets with ease and comfort. The famous Questar and Meade ETX line are among the most well known.

These telescopes will be the best in terms of size-to-quality ratio, but also the most expensive. Be reasonably sure the person you are buying the scope for will likely take a serious interest in the hobby. Unless of course money is no object, in which case buy one of these and please put me in your will.

This is also a place where the telescope market is changing. Thanks to cost savings on Dobsonian mounts, some SCT telescopes with tracking motors can now be purchased for little more than the price of a Newtonian Dobsonian.

Telescope Mounts

As covered in the first chapter, the telescope mount is absolutely critical, but often this is overlooked.

Classic tripods, especially small, light ones, are rarely good telescope mounts.

Personally, I have never found a tripod on a small scope that was not at minimum a frustration to use, unless it was part of a motorized fork mount. Some older style 4 and 5-inch Newtonian telescopes had sturdy tripods, but were unwieldy and required some practice to use well.

The best mounts for lower-priced grab-and-go beginner telescopes are Dobsonian mounts or a Dobsonian modified for tabletop use.

The best mounts for higher-end grab-and-go telescopes are motorized fork mounts integrated into a tripod or Dobsonian base.

So what are Dobsonians?

John Dobson (1915-2014) was one of the most important amateur astronomers to ever have lived, having more impact on our hobby than almost any single person since Messier, Hershel, or Newton. Yet John Dobson did not discover any new stars, galaxies or comets.

John Dobson was a star-gazing monk, living in a monastery. Because of his vows of poverty, he could not buy a telescope. Using cast-off materials, he single-handedly built his telescopes from scratch, inventing an entirely new mounting and control system that is both affordable and highly effective. He went on to create the "Sidewalk Astronomy" movement and recreated the hobby of building your own telescopes from scratch. His methods not only brought telescope ownership to beginners in a new and revolutionary way, but also allowed people to build or buy telescopes of the size and quality that previously only observatories and universities could afford.

Dobson would spend hundreds of hours sourcing free scrap materials, bringing them back to the monastery to tirelessly build telescopes with optics that were on par with some of the finest commercially available. He would take the telescopes into the city at night, set up on a sidewalk, and show anyone that would care to look a view of the planets and the stars. If someone was particularly interested in astronomy, he would GIVE them his telescope and set off to build another.

The telescopes using the mounting technology Dobson invented are called Dobsonians.

To date, no other telescope mount offers more bang-for-the-buck, or more intuitive easy-to-learn operation and handling than a Dobsonian. Additionally, Dobsonian telescopes, if well made are reasonably portable and highly durable.

Other than that, they are just "ok".

Dobsonian designs allow amateurs to have large scopes that are reasonably transportable. This one, owned by George Riley, is a Push-To truss Dobsonian.

Until recently, the principle shortcoming of Dobsonian telescopes was the inability track the stars as they moved across the sky. The Dobsonian user had to use an eyepiece with a wide field-of-view and move the telescope by hand to follow the target in the sky.

New motor drives that work a platform that the telescope is placed on, or that rotate the base and move the telescope up and down, are now available as commercial products, but unfortunately the price has yet to come down enough for them to qualify as budget beginner telescopes. At the time of this writing, a few Dobsonians with motorized tracking are available for just under $250 and provide a wonderful balance of portability, usability and cost.

What do Dobsonians have to do with beginner telescopes?

Just as Dobson's invention allowed amateurs to have large observatory-quality telescopes affordably, it also allowed beginners to have affordable, high-quality, easy-to-use introductory telescopes.

Dobsonian bases not only work better and are easier to use for a beginner, but also cost far less to manufacture. They can be a bit bulky to ship and transport, but if you are willing to supply a sturdy table, the tabletop, Dobsonian-like telescopes are some of the best starter and grab-and-go instruments.

If you are willing to commit some additional room for storing and transporting your telescope, 6-inch basic Dobsonian telescopes are easy to use telescopes, with the largest aperture, in the affordable beginner market.

Manual, Motorized Tracking, Push-To Computerized and GoTo Computerized Mounts

The four types of telescope mount control are confusing for beginners.

Manual only mounts require the user to move the telescope to locate a target and to periodically move the mount to re-center the target as the earth rotates.

Motorized mounts require the user to move the telescope to locate a target. After the target is found the mount drive motors will keep the target in the eyepiece. Using motors to keep the target in the eyepiece is called "Tracking." Initial setup requires the user to level the telescope and point it North.

PushTo computerized mounts require the user to move the telescope to locate a target. The computer assists the user in finding the target by indicating the direction the user needs to push the scope to find the target. Push-To mounts have no motors so they cannot track. The computer in a PushTo mount must be manually aligned before use.

GoTo mounts have a computer and motors that can move the scope to find targets automatically and once found, can track the targets as the earth rotates. Usually GoTo mounts will have a hand controller and require an alignment process before they can be used.

More about GoTo Telescope Mounts

GoTo telescopes have motorized mounts with a computer controller that not only holds the object being viewed in the eyepiece as the earth rotates, but also quickly points to any object in the sky automatically.

Almost every internet discussion forum has a long ongoing debate among its members as to whether beginners should use a computerized scope or a manual scope as a first telescope.

Those advocating having manual telescope mounts contend that learning the sky, being able to identify the constellations and to use a chart to star-hop to an object is an important beginners skill.

Those advocating having GoTo telescopes for beginners point out that beginners may become frustrated at learning charts, that objects in light-polluted skies are often hard to find manually and that you can always turn off the GoTo if you want to learn to star hop.

The first thing to consider is if you can afford a GoTo telescope.

GoTo telescopes START at a little more than twice the price of a good manual telescope. At the time of this writing, that is about $300 US.

The second thing to know about GoTo telescopes is that you will still have to know how to align the telescope to the night sky. For most people, this will take several tries during the first night's practice session to learn and get right.

The moon and planets are easy to find, and aligning the telescope to just find the moon and planets is mostly a waste of time. However, the tracking function of GoTo scopes that keeps the planet centered in the eyepiece for long periods of time likely makes the effort of alignment worthwhile.

If you are primarily planning on viewing the moon and planets the extra cost of a GoTo is not likely justified.

More about PushTo Telescope Mounts

PushTo telescopes do not move the telescope to objects in the sky for you, but they do help you find them.

If you plan on going hunting for more difficult to view objects, GoTo or PushTo can be a huge help, especially in light polluted suburban skies or if you do not enjoy the challenge of star hopping.

Remember that with a GoTo or PushTo scope you will have to do a 2 to 3 minute alignment before each viewing session. The alignment typically consists of entering your time and location, then pointing the telescope at two of the brightest stars in the sky. The accuracy of this alignment directly affects how well the GoTo or PushTo system will work.

So where did we end up?

If you want a good-performing telescope that is very transportable (grab-and-go) at the low end of the cost range, a tabletop reflector (aka mini-Dobsonian) is a very good bet. If you are willing to take the time to shop carefully, some tabletop refractors are also very nice instruments.

This Mak-Cassegrain, on a motorized Dobsonian base, is an example of the tabletop revolution. This amazing little telescope has great optics, wonderful sturdy mount characteristics and does motorized tracking. With an upgrade, this scope can also do computerized GoTo. The price, at the time of this book's publication, was less than $250. A scope like this has all of the qualities of a great first telescope or a Grab-and-Go for experienced hobbyists.

If you are willing to give up some space and portability, 4-6 inch Dobsonian reflectors are easy to use and gather a great deal of light for the price.

At the high end of the price spectrum, Schmidt Cassegrain and Maksutov Cassegrain telescopes from 90mm to 125mm with GoTo computerized bases are the all-time favorite grab-and-go telescopes by people of all skill levels.

Review of important terms:

Tracking: The ability of a telescope to keep an object in the eyepiece view, over time, as the Earth rotates.

PushTo: A computerized telescope that helps you find objects in the sky, but does not track or GoTo.

GoTo: A computerized telescope that will automatically move the telescope to an object in the sky and will track the object as the Earth rotates.

Alignment: The procedure that teaches the telescope its time, date, location and position allowing it to GoTo or PushTo. This typically takes a few minutes and requires the user of the telescope to know two bright stars visible in the sky.

6 SELECTING A GOOD ASTRONOMY GUIDE

"The vastness of the heavens stretches my imagination…stuck on this carousel, my little eye can catch one-million-year-old light. A vast pattern… of which I am a part… What is the pattern or the meaning, or the why? It does not do harm to the mystery to know a little more about it. For far more marvelous is the truth, than any artists of the past imagined it."
-Richard Feynman

In chapter 2, we found many guides are misleading for those that observe under suburban or urban skies. Thankfully, however, a number of good books and websites do have information partly or wholly written for the suburban or urban observer.

Thanks to the information age, we are also not limited to static information and guides. Computer software, and tablet/phone apps can be extremely helpful guides to the night sky.

If a book or webpage does not expressly say it is a guide for urban astronomy, check the object descriptions, especially galaxies and nebulae entries, to see if they describe the viewing conditions necessary to view the object with a light-pollution grade. Also, sketches or black and white photos are a good sign and detailed color photographs of the objects are a bad sign.

Light-pollution grades might be described in general terms such as Dark Skies Steady, Dark Skies, Suburban, and Urban. Or, the grades might be described in very specific terms using the "Bortle scale."

John E. Bortle created a scale that can be used to rate light-pollution at most locations around the world. A number of web pages and applications have overlay maps to help find where on the 1 through 9 scale your location rates on the Bortle scale.

In some locations, part of your visible sky in one direction may have more light-pollution than another direction because one direction is toward a city and the other toward open country or water. Being able to plan your observations by looking for objects that will be in better areas of your sky can be helpful.

Light-pollution is a big factor, but there is also another important factor to consider —the seeing conditions or astronomy weather for the night.

By using your internet search engine to query "Astronomy Weather" you should find several good web services that rate the local weather on such attributes as Cloud Cover, Transparency, Seeing, Darkness, Wind, Humidity, and Temperature.

If your transparency is very good, the effects of suburban light-pollution will be greatly diminished (and vice versa). If humidity is high, you will likely need dew-caps or dew-heaters. Good seeing conditions help seeing detail on planets.

On very humid nights, bright objects will appear to have halos and planetary details will be lost. This is a realistic view of Jupiter and some of its moons

through a 90mm telescope. If this was a good-seeing night, the coma would be gone and some cloud banding might be visible on Jupiter.

One of the most popular places to find this forecast information is Clear Sky Chart at www.ClearDarkSky.com or one of the mobile apps that query this site's data.

We know about bad guides, we know about the weather; what next?

Chapter one let us know not to expect full-color Hubble-like images through our backyard telescopes. So why do so many people go crazy for backyard astronomy?

If you can just pick up a DVD or a photo book full of Hubble telescope photos that are much more colorful and detailed than viewed through a telescope with the naked eye, why bother buying a telescope?

When these questions are asked to amateur astronomers, the responses overwhelmingly include descriptions about how seeing the <u>real objects</u> with one's own eyes, and especially knowing something about the objects such as size, distance and significance, make the experience far more rewarding than a photo or video.

Supposing the previous paragraph is reasonably true, then telescope purchases are enhanced by learning about the objects that will be observed.

Planning an Observing Session

Taking some time to find out what is going to be in the night sky that you can see from your location with your equipment and weather is important to successfully finding objects. Equally important is pre-researching for knowledge is the power to fully appreciate what you find.

If you plan to hunt down a comet, perhaps spend some nights, when the moon or clouds prevent viewing, catching up on reading Carl Sagan's book *Comet*. If you are going to be viewing Jupiter or Saturn, perhaps some documentary videos or a good book would be helpful, and the same principle applies to deep-sky objects as well.

Many hobbyists also report that logging and especially sketching what they view, adds a great deal to their enjoyment, allowing them to notice more detail and features than they normally would.

Sketching-form templates can be found on the internet using the search phrase "astronomy sketch template." I use forms from the American Association of Amateur Astronomers.

Some astronomy guides combine information on when and where the objects in the sky can be viewed, under what conditions they can be viewed and what equipment can be used while also describing the objects' attributes with realistic sketches rather than Hubble photographs. These guides are uncommon but valuable and as you would expect, cherished by experienced and new astronomers alike.

One astronomy guide that exemplifies the above is titled *Turn Left at Orion*. This is one of the best print guides available (there is also a Kindle version) and would be a great book to buy after you finish reading this one, or to gift with a telescope.

***Turn Left At Orion* is one of the best astronomy guides. It uses sketches to**

portray what you will see through the telescope, not color photos.

Many new guides are "Apps," programs for mobile smartphones and tablets. A few examples of interesting apps will be listed in this book but remember that things change and these apps could be very different or perhaps not even available by the time you read this. Therefore, for this book to be useful to you, look for applications with similar features rather than just the exact applications used as examples in this book.

Presently, *SkySafari*, *Stellarium* and *UniverseHD* are among some of the best tablet applications available for amateur astronomers. These applications help you navigate the night sky, plan observing sessions, learn about objects, and log observations; and they update themselves with new information about comets and other events. Some of these applications can even be used to control computerized telescopes.

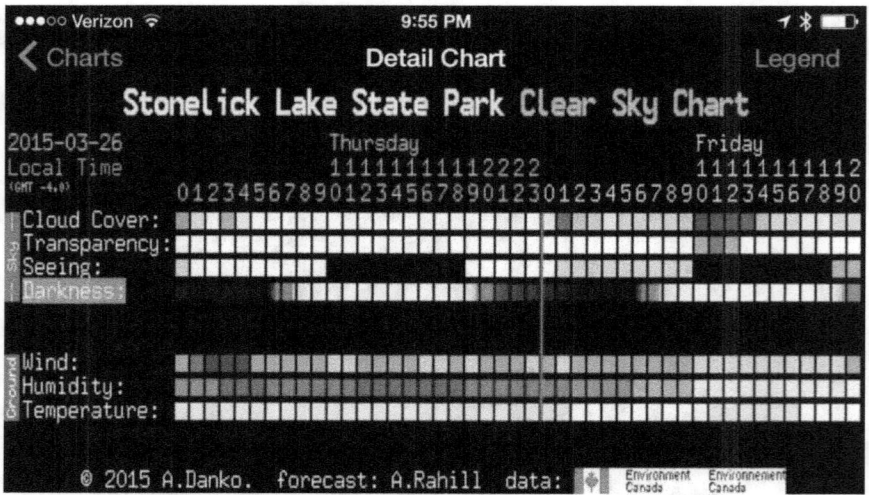

There is more to consider than clouds when looking at weather for astronomy. "Clear Sky Charts" are very popular.

Currently these applications do not do a good job of forecasting local weather nor of looking up the degree of light-pollution on the Bortle scale. *Scope Nights* is a good application for astronomy weather as well as *myCSC* and *Moon Calendar*.

Screenshot from the smartphone app *Scope Nights* showing the viewing weather forecast.

For finding Jupiter's Great Red Spot and identifying the moons of Jupiter and Saturn, *JupiterMoons* and *Gas Giants* are wonderful apps.

Smartphone apps, like *Jupiter Moons* are great for discovering when the Great Red Spot will be visible.

For aligning motorized or computerized telescopes there are lots of apps to help find your exact time and location including *Astro Kit*, *GPSCompass*, *AstroSky*, *AstroClock* and *Scope Help*.

Back to the Moon

The moon influences or controls the tides, biological rhythms, mythology and amateur astronomy.

Moonlight will wash out faint deep-sky objects, the effect becoming even worse during poor-transparency nights and light polluted locations. Therefore, when the moon is in its brighter stages you may consider making the moon your target for observations.

Many people like a list to follow, or a challenge, so you might consider a list of moon locations to tour. Many astronomers like to keep a log of the objects or features they "bag" while making observations.

The moon holds many surprising and wonderful features.

Sir (as in he got knighted for doing this sort of thing) Patrick Moore was such a good amateur observer of the moon, NASA came to HIM for lunar advice on the Apollo missions!

Sir Patrick Moore hosted a BBC television show for amateur astronomers, and would publish a "Moore Marathon" in which he would challenge amateurs from ALL skill levels and equipment types (even naked eye) to try to bag a number of items on his lists.

The "Moore Moon Marathon," a collection of five guides, is an excellent starter for anyone interested in astronomy, even for those with little or no equipment or experience. Unfortunately, the BBC has not made these guides easy to find on the internet. Some internet searching should eventually lead you to find .pdf versions of these fantastic guides. If you cannot find these guides on the internet, email the author of this book for a link.

"Moore Moon Marathon" guides:

1. The Lunar Seas

2. Bright and Dark Craters
3. Craters in Shadow
4. Majestic Mountains
5. Lunar Specials

For a longer list and more granular targets, research "The Lunar 100" published by "Landsend Astronomers." They provide free guides, maps and journals for lunar observations.

Previously recommended, *Turn Left at Orion* is also a first class guide to lunar observing.

Free high resolution downloadable moon maps are provided by the USGS and can be accessed here:
http://pubs.usgs.gov/sim/3316/

The next guide to observing is so good and so useful that the entire next chapter is dedicated to it. See you there!

7 CLUBS, FORUMS AND OUTREACH

"The value of a telescope is not determined by what you paid for it. Its value comes from how many people have looked through it."

-John Dobson

The very best guides to amateur astronomy are fellow amateur astronomers.

If you are fortunate, you live in a city or region that has one or more astronomy societies, organizations, or clubs. If not internet organizations can also be invaluable.

Having a club or friends in the amateur astronomy hobby is extremely helpful, presenting opportunities to try out new equipment and to see objects that you might not have considered hunting down yourself.

Some clubs are made up mostly of members who do not own telescopes but enjoy programs hosted by the club. The size, resources and programs available in an organization can vary greatly.

Some organizations have been sponsored by, or work with, observatories and or planetariums. This expands the resources of the club exponentially and typically is a bonus for both organizations. In many cases, the club gets space for meetings or events and perhaps some equipment usage and the institution expands its exposure and volunteer base.

Dark Sites

A popular and highly desirable feature that some astronomy clubs have is a "dark-sky site". The definition of what a dark-sky site is can vary greatly, but in some way it is a location available to the club that has less light-pollution than the average club member's backyard.

Clubs with substantial resources may own land outside of town that they use as a dark site. Another strategy that some clubs use is to partner with a national, state or local park to use an area on specific nights for club or public viewing.

One of the advantages to partnering with a park or nature center to provide dark site access is that a parking lot or other paved hard surface might be available. Hard surfaces, especially those near or in a parking lot, allow equipment to be easily setup, avoids soft, wet ground and generally provides better access for everyone.

A disadvantage to partnering with a park or nature center is the difficulty ensuring that an area is free of lights. Make certain that any agreement is documented so that a change in park management does not upend the agreement.

When visiting a dark site there are several things to keep in mind as a courtesy to those around you:

1. LIGHT: Use flashlights as little as possible. If you do use them make sure they are dim and preferably have a red colored lens.

2. ASK: Always ask before looking through a telescope.

3. RESPECT: Be sure that you, your friends and especially children with you know not to move or touch the body of someone else's telescope, but to just look through the eyepiece.

Public Events and Outreach

Many clubs will sponsor public events or outreach programs for the community. During special celestial events such as eclipses, transits and meteor showers, many clubs will have open houses.

These are fantastic opportunities to get exposed to amateur astronomy and to review equipment before purchasing.

Some clubs and observatories will have programs that, after you complete a short class, will allow you to borrow and take home equipment similar to checking out a library book. This is another golden opportunity to get to use equipment before a purchase. Other clubs may have equipment that you can use on premises, after a "check out" or training session.

Once you have mastered your equipment, you may want to consider returning the favor by taking your equipment to an outreach event to share with others.

Eric Harris, shocked by a bright flash from the camera, is using a club telescope to do photography as well as public-event outreach. His demonstrations at public events have influenced others to purchase telescopes.

Online Forums

The internet has many wonderful features and one of them is online astronomy forums.

With online forums you can research beginner equipment and ask questions that you have not found answers to elsewhere. Forums come and go and have various cultures and user-bases, but most astronomy forums are highly welcoming and supportive of beginners.

Without a local club, online forums might be your only avenue to get support from other amateur astronomers.

Typically, forums require you to register if you want to post (ask a question), but not to just lurk (read). Forums will have topics or sections that pertain to particular specialties such as sketching or astrophotography. As a beginner, you should introduce yourself and ask your questions in the beginners' section.

If you ask a question in an online forum, expect conflicting answers. One skill you will soon acquire after using online forums is determining which replies are most helpful, just like when you ask a group of people questions in the real world.

Online forums typically allow you to search topics after registering. This search function allows you to research equipment, events and anything related to the forums. The term "First Light" is often used by people to describe a post about their first experience with a new telescope or other equipment.

Internet forums sometimes last for decades, others come and go. At the time of this writing a few of the more popular and active forums include:

AstronomyForum.net (noted for a friendly atmosphere, USA centric)

CloudyNights.com (famous for equipment reviews and classified ads)

StargazersLounge.com (UK/International)

AstroMart (mostly used-equipment classifieds)

8 IMPROVING YOUR OBSERVING

When observing with any telescope, but especially a small telescope under suburban skies, you want as many advantages as possible.

One FREE way to make your telescope perform many times better is to let your eyes adapt to the dark, improving your "night vision."

As you learned in biology class, your eyes have two photoreceptive cells, rods and cones. Cones adapt to the dark in about 10 minutes and rods after about 20-45 minutes.

Dark-adapted eyes cannot only see dim objects in a telescope much better, but also telescope knobs and controls. Any flash of bright light, even for an instant, sets your eyes back to zero and you have to start adapting all over again.

This is why amateur astronomers try to avoid using flashlights, or use dim red flashlights. Red flashlights are easy to make, but understand the most important quality is that the light be dim.

When selecting a place to view the night sky, obviously you will want a place with a good unobstructed, view of the heavens. The next aspect to evaluate is stray light. A neighbor's bright porch light, or a street light shining directly at you will greatly reduce your ability to observe.

If you are unable to turn off the offending lights, try blocking the light or moving to a location that reduces the amount of light directly shining on you.

Additionally, you will want to be comfortable. Give some thought to the seating, temperature, drinks, snacks and clear paths to restrooms. You won't want to lose your night vision upon entering the house on an errand so pre-plan some dim lighting indoors. Also protect outdoor lighting by closing the shades so family members don't turn on room lights that shine into the yard.

Some amateur astronomers will wear an eye patch when using a flashlight or when going into the house to preserve night vision in one eye.

Eye Glasses

If you wear glasses, typically you will want to leave them ON when observing through an eyepiece. With some eye conditions, you can refocus the telescope eyepiece to get around using your glasses but this is not always possible.

If you wear glasses, you should shop for telescope eyepieces that advertise a large "eye relief." Eye relief is the room between your eye and the eyepiece lens. If you wear glasses, you want enough eye relief to give room for your glasses.

Averted Vision

Averted vision helps when viewing dim or faint objects through a telescope. It seems strange, but it does work well, especially with practice.

The technique is to look around an object, NOT directly at it. This technique, as strange as it seems, allows your eye to pick out much more detail.

Sometimes gentle scope-rocking can also help you see a dim object, just be careful not to move the scope away from the object.

9 BINOCULARS

Binoculars? Is this not a telescope book?

Binoculars are excellent astronomy tools, although they don't get as much good press as telescopes. They are sort of the Rodney Dangerfield of the telescope world. That said, they do have a dedicated following.

Binoculars can be used for astronomy as long as they have at least a 50mm aperture. The standard binocular description is "magnification X aperture" (example 10x50 is 10 magnification by 50mm).

Why is the minimum recommended aperture for binoculars 50mm when for telescopes it is 90mm? Binoculars bring 50mm of light into both eyes at once, so they have the effect of almost 100mm.

Binoculars excel at giving a very wide field-of-view at low magnification. So, for comets and open star clusters they perform better than almost all telescopes. They are also very good for observing the Andromeda galaxy and for lunar observation.

If you have a set of common 7x50, 10x50, or larger binoculars sitting in your closet you already have a wonderful astronomy tool you can start using tonight.

7x50 or 10x50 binoculars make excellent wide-field viewing scopes when mounted to a tripod. This set was brought to a public-viewing session by amateur astronomer Jeff Mancini.

The principle drawback to binoculars is that they are fixed at one magnification. Some zoom binoculars are available on the market but, they tend to have collimation (alignment) problems, which is very bad for astronomy use.

Using Binoculars

Before using binoculars for astronomy you should take some time during the day to make sure they are clean and that each side of the binoculars are parafocal (both sides come to focus at the same point). Most binoculars have one eyepiece that turns, allowing you to adjust the optics to bring both sides into focus. You will also want to get an idea on how far apart the eyepieces should be so that you don't see double.

For smaller binoculars, find a comfortable place to rest your arms while looking up at the night sky. After a few minutes of holding binoculars above your head, it will be surprising how heavy they feel.

For larger binoculars, you will want a tripod, or even better, a parallelogram mount.

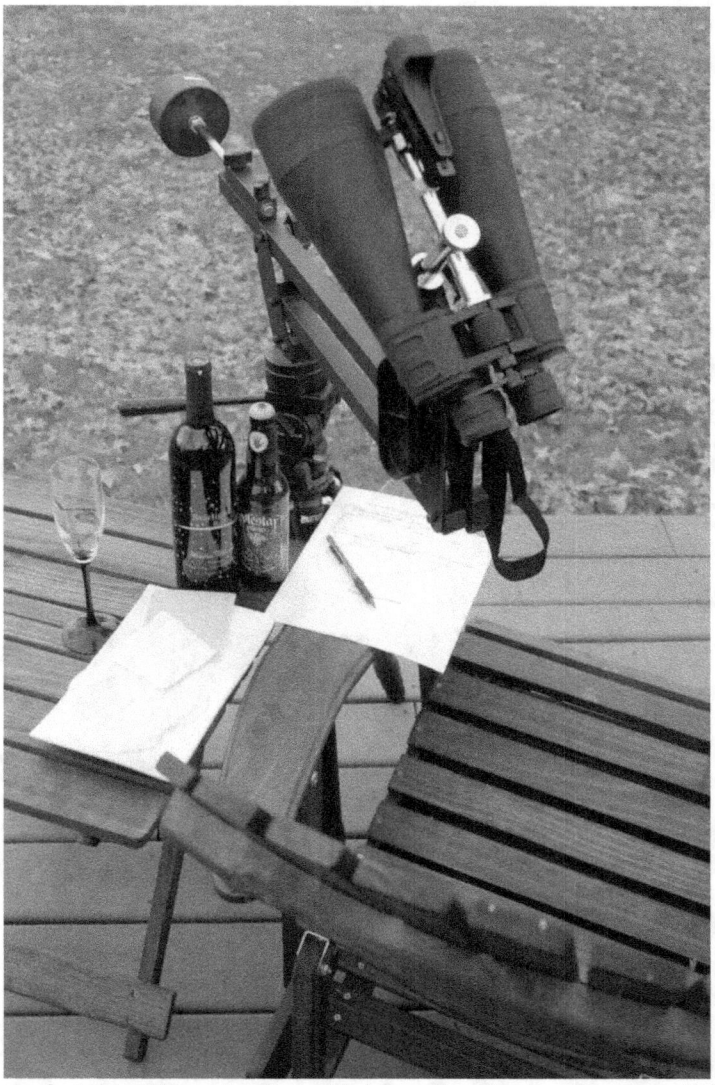

Being comfortable when viewing with binoculars is a must. A parallelogram mount is necessary for larger binoculars.

Binoculars can also make a great companion to telescopes, as you can find some objects like star clusters first by star hopping with the binoculars then repeating the process with your telescope. The wide field-of-view with binoculars can also help with identifying larger structures on the moon.

10 GO GET A TELESCOPE!

If this book gets any larger it is going to turn into a beginner's guide instead of a guide to beginner's guides!

So please get out there and use some critical thinking to avoid bad marketing. Take the advice in this book and other good guides, to find a worthy 90mm or larger telescope with a good mount.

Remember the best or most valuable scope is not the largest or the most costly, but the one that is used most often.

Should this hobby take off for you, please take the time to help others also discover the night sky.

I wish you clear skies!

Recommended Resources Available at the Time of Publishing:

Blogs:

Polluted Skies Stargazing is a wonderful site by Luis Carvajal that documents wonderful sky events with sketches made through binoculars. http://pollutedskiesstargazing.blogspot.com/

Astro Bob is a blog kept by a famous astronomy writer that wonderfully documents news and events under the title "Celestial happenings you can see from your own backyard".

http://astrobob.areavoices.com/

The Urban Astronomer also has a blog well suited to suburban backyard viewing.
http://urbanastronomer.blogspot.com/

Publications:

Sky and Telescope
http://www.skyandtelescope.com/

BBC Sky at Night
http://www.skyatnightmagazine.com/

Astronomy Magazine
http://www.astronomy.com/

PodCasts

StarTalk
http://www.startalkradio.net/

Astronomy Cast
http://www.astronomycast.com/

Weather

Clear Sky
http://cleardarksky.com/csk/

Intellicast
http://www.intellicast.com/National/Outdoors/Sky.aspx

NOAA
http://graphical.weather.gov/sectors/conus.php?element=Sky

Planning

Sky Tonight
http://tonightssky.com/MainPage.php

Sketching Forms, American Association of Amateur Astronomers
http://www.astromax.org/aa02801.htm

ABOUT THE AUTHOR

Timothy O'Connor has been active in amateur astronomy for approximately twenty-five years. He can be found doing public astronomy outreach at events in Southern Ohio and Northern Kentucky. Tim has published two other introductory books, *You Can Afford to be a Pilot* and *Dogs Ride*.

Tim has made a living for the past twenty years in computer networking, security and technical training. Tim holds some of the highest certifications in the computer training industry and is a certified flight instructor. Tim holds numerous pilot ratings including Advanced Ground Instructor, Commercial Rotorcraft pilot, and FAA Fast Team Safety Volunteer.

In addition to technical training and consulting, Tim co-hosted a top-rated radio show for three years on WNOP and has written cover and feature articles for such publications as ROTORCRAFT, EAA Sport Pilot, Sport Aviation, The Experimenter, Light Plane World, Homebuilt Rotorcraft, Powered Sport Flying, The Utopian and has published content in AVWeb, Technology First, jp4 and other publications.

www.ingramcontent.com/pod-product-compliance
Lightning Source LLC
Chambersburg PA
CBHW071225280526
45787CB00002B/815